Devin Hester

Jeff C. Young
AR B.L.: 6.7 Alt.: 1019
Points: 2.0

MG

SUPERSTARS
of
PRO FOOTBALL

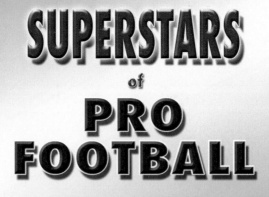

Jeff C. Young

Mason Crest Publishers

BOOK DEDICATION — To Brad Gates, a strong survivor.

Produced by OTTN Publishing in association with
21st Century Publishing and Communications, Inc.

MASON CREST PUBLISHERS INC.
370 Reed Road
Broomall, Pennsylvania 19008
(866) MCP-BOOK (toll free)
www.masoncrest.com

Printed in the United States of America.

First Printing

9 8 7 6 5 4 3 2 1

Library of Congress Cataloging-in-Publication Data

Young, Jeff C., 1948–
    Devin Hester / Jeff C. Young.
        p. cm. — (Superstars of pro football)
    Includes bibliographical references.
ISBN-13: 978-1-4222-0545-7 (hardcover) — ISBN-10: 1-4222-0545-2 (hardcover)
ISBN-13: 978-1-4222-0825-0 (pbk.) — ISBN-10: 1-4222-0825-7 (pbk.)
    1. Hester, Devin, 1982–   —Juvenile literature. 2. Football players—United States—
Biography—Juvenile literature. I. Title.
GV939.H47Y68 2008
796.332092—dc22
[B]   2008024548

Publisher's note:
All quotations in this book come from original sources, and contain the spelling
and grammatical inconsistencies of the original text.

◀◀ CROSS-CURRENTS ▶▶

In the ebb and flow of the currents of life we are each influenced
by many people, places, and events that we directly experience or
have learned about. Throughout the chapters of this book you will
come across **CROSS-CURRENTS** reference bubbles. These bubbles
direct you to a **CROSS-CURRENTS** section in the back of the
book that contains fascinating and informative sidebars
and related pictures. Go on. ▶▶

◀◀CONTENTS▶▶

AN EXPLOSIVE YOUNG PLAYER

During the 2006 National Football League (NFL) season, a player named Devin Hester achieved an unusual feat. It was only Devin's first season playing in the NFL, but he was selected to play in the 2007 Pro Bowl, an annual all-star game that features the NFL's best players. It's rare for a rookie to make the Pro Bowl team!

During the 2006 season, Devin had proven he was an outstanding **kick returner**. He returned five kicks for touchdowns that season, and he was voted **Special Teams** Player of the Week in the National Football Conference (NFC) three times. In December 2006, Devin was named the NFC's Player of the Month.

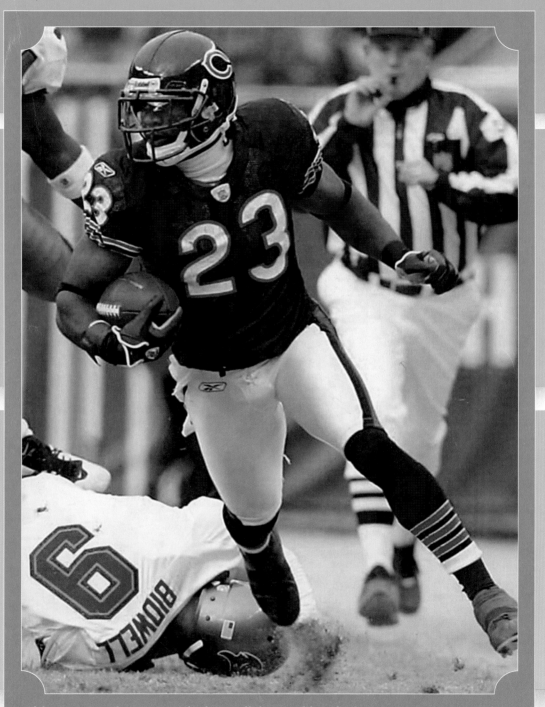

Chicago's Devin Hester eludes a diving tackler during a 2006 game against the Tampa Bay Buccaneers. In his rookie year, Devin emerged as one of the NFL's most exciting players. He scored five times on kick returns.

One particularly memorable play of 2006 came during a game against the New York Giants. Devin, standing in the end zone, caught a missed 52-yard **field goal** attempt by the Giants. He ran the ball back 108 yards to score a touchdown.

Devin's strong play helped his team, the Chicago Bears, reach the Super Bowl, the NFL's championship game. During Super Bowl XLI in February 2007, Devin returned the first kick of the game 92 yards for a touchdown. It was the first time in Super Bowl history that a player had scored on the opening **kickoff**.

The Pro Bowl was held one week after that Super Bowl. Devin showed he deserved to be on the NFC's team. During the Pro Bowl, he returned four kickoffs for a total of 97 yards. His longest kickoff return in that game was 33 yards.

CROSS-CURRENTS

To learn more about the history of the NFL's annual all-star game, check out "The Pro Bowl." Go to page 46. ▶▶

Devin also made an exciting **punt** return that captured everyone's attention. Midway through the fourth quarter, Devin caught a high, spiraling punt on his team's 14-yard line. Devin faked left, then quickly cut back to the right. As he ran up the field, he made two more cuts, pretended to toss the ball to another player, and broke two tackles.

Finally, LaDainian Tomlinson of the American Football Conference (AFC) San Diego Chargers tackled Devin at the AFC's 22-yard line to stop him from making a touchdown. Although the NFC lost the 2007 Pro Bowl, 31–28, Devin's punt return was one of the game's highlights.

Best in the League

Devin continued his strong play into the 2007 season—his second in the NFL. Even though many teams refused to kick the ball toward his side of the field, Devin still returned six kicks for touchdowns to set a new league record.

Devin's explosiveness led the Bears to use him as a **wide receiver** on offense. In 2007, Devin had 20 catches and averaged 15 yards per reception as a wide receiver. He also scored two touchdowns as a receiver. One of these touchdowns came on on an 81-yard run.

Devin's quickness and ability left his opponents stunned and his teammates impressed. After one 2007 game in which Devin returned

Devin breaks away for a 92-yard touchdown on the opening kickoff of Super Bowl XLI, February 4, 2007. Although Devin's brilliant return gave the Bears a quick 7–0 lead, the Indianapolis Colts came back to win, 29–17.

two kicks to score two touchdowns, fellow Bears receiver Rashied Davis told *USA Today*:

❝I'm not amazed any more. I'm amazed when they kick it to him. I know the more they kick it to him, the more likely he's going to take it to the house [to score a touchdown].❞

As a result, Devin was among the NFC's top ten vote getters in the selection for the 2008 Pro Bowl team. He was the only kick returner to make the top ten. In an article published before the Pro Bowl, ESPN sportswriter Mike McCallister described Devin's strengths:

CROSS-CURRENTS

Read "Pro Bowl Rules" to learn how this all-star exhibition game is not like NFL games played during the regular season. Go to page 47. ▶▶

During the 2008 Pro Bowl, Devin had kickoff returns of 51, 25, and 36 yards. Devin ran another kickoff back 14 yards before tossing the ball to teammate Jason Witten, who picked up an additional 35 yards.

"Hester is the quick, shifty return guy, the one who can stop on a dime, find space that seemingly doesn't exist, and slip around the grasp of lunging opponents. That works best in crowded situations, such as on punt returns, where the players are on top of him as he fields the ball."

Improving with Time

After just two seasons in the NFL, Devin established himself as one of the league's most explosive and dangerous players. Every time he touches the ball, he is a threat to score a touchdown. His 11 career touchdowns on kickoff and punt returns rank him fourth all-time among NFL players. The three players ahead of him on the list all played for many years, and yet Devin's numbers came after only two seasons. It seems likely that Devin will eventually rank number one in kick returns for touchdowns.

Bears coaches, players, and fans hope that as Devin gains more experience, he will play more as a starting wide receiver. As a wide receiver, Devin can have an even larger role in the team's offense. During a 2008 training camp meeting, Darryl Drake, the coach of the Bears' wide receivers, told the *Chicago Sun-Times,*

"I have been around a lot of guys, a lot of really good receivers, and he has a chance to be better than all of them. . . . He has as good a pair of hands as anybody. And then his natural ability to run after the catch is just unbelievable. He has not dropped a ball. Not one ball in any of these practices. . . . I don't have to tell him anything anymore. . . . he's just so far ahead right now it's unbelievable."

Devin may be ahead of his game now, but it was a long road to get there. Devin's family and his love of sports helped him along the way.

A ROUGH START

Before learning to carry a football, Devin Hester learned to carry burdens in his life. Devin was born on November 4, 1982, in Riviera Beach, Florida. His parents, Lenorris Hester Sr. and Juanita Brown, divorced shortly after Devin was born. His father, his stepfather Derrick Brown, his mother, and his older brother Lenorris Jr. all helped with Devin's upbringing.

While he was growing up, Devin experienced several family tragedies. When he was 10, his mother Juanita was severely injured in a car accident. Juanita was nearly paralyzed and was bedridden for a long time.

Two years after his mother's accident, Devin's father died of cancer at the age of 33. Devin has never spoken publicly about the pain and grief caused by his father's death. His older brother Lenorris Jr. spoke for both himself and Devin when he said:

> **"It was probably the worst pain that me and him have felt. . . . He [Lenorris Sr.] said he knew he wasn't going to be here. He told me and Devin to go into the world and be somebody. That stuck with us."**

Devin Hester did not have an easy childhood. His mother was badly hurt in an accident, and his father died at a young age. Devin also struggled with his grades in school.

An Early Start

Derrick and Lenorris Jr. felt Devin could escape his depression and grief by playing sports. Devin was 11 when he started playing football in a youth league. As a boy, Devin **idolized** Deion "Prime Time" Sanders, an NFL kick returner and defensive back. Devin set out to become like Deion, a player who could break a game open with his speed and shifty moves.

Devin later described how, when he scored his first touchdown in a youth league game, he started running like Deion Sanders:

CROSS-CURRENTS

To learn more about the life and career of one of Devin's favorite players, read "Deion 'Prime Time' Sanders." Go to page 48. ▶▶

"I was 11, playing linebacker . . . and I got a pick on the first play of the game. I wanted to do Deion's thing. My first time playing organized football, and I was high-stepping it!"

Devin went on to play football at Suncoast Community High School, a school better known for its academics than its athletics. Suncoast had earned a national ranking in the Academic Games competition.

On Suncoast's team, Devin played cornerback on defense and was a running back, wide receiver, and kick return specialist on offense. Devin's high school coach, Jimmie Bell, remembers that he played Devin "wherever I could put him."

Suncoast's team won just three games during Devin's senior year—but the team's losses didn't reflect how well Devin played. As a running back, he ran for 1,014 yards on 94 carries—an outstanding average of 10.8 yards per carry! He also scored 12 rushing touchdowns. As a receiver, Devin caught 38 passes for 1,028 yards and nine touchdowns. Devin even threw five touchdown passes.

Devin's offensive achievements, however, only tell half the story. On defense, Devin made 156 tackles (75 unassisted) and had three quarterback **sacks**. He also caused three **fumbles** and had one fumble recovery. As a result, Devin was named to the All-State Team.

All-Around All-American

Devin's sensational senior year made him a great college **prospect**. *Parade Magazine* named him to its High School All-American team,

Deion Sanders, shown here playing with the San Francisco 49ers in 1995, was one of Devin's favorite players. Sanders, an all-star defensive player, was nicknamed "Prime Time" because of his ability to make big plays.

and *USA Today* named Devin a First-Team High School All-American. The *Miami Herald* ranked him as the number two prospect in Florida and the number eight prospect in the nation.

Football wasn't the only sport in which Devin earned All-American honors. His speed and leaping ability made him a standout in track and field as well. While still in high school, Devin was clocked at 4.33 seconds in the 40-yard dash, and his vertical leap measured 38 inches. As a long jumper, Devin was ranked second in the nation during his junior year. Devin's long-jumping skills made him a two-sport high school All-American.

Devin's rank as a top college football prospect was enhanced by a spectacular play he made in the CaliFlorida Bowl. This postseason all-star game features the best high school players from California and Florida. During the game, Devin scored a touchdown on an

The Miami Hurricanes celebrate during a 2002 game. During Devin's senior year in high school, the Hurricanes were ranked second in the nation. Devin agreed to play football at Miami, hoping for the chance to play for a national championship.

85-yard kickoff return. He also **intercepted** a pass and made three tackles on defense.

Devin was voted the game's Most Valuable Player. There was no longer any question whether Devin was going to play football at a major university. The only question was which university.

Making A Choice

When Devin graduated from Suncoast, three Florida universities were noted for their outstanding football teams. The University of Florida, Florida State University, and the University of Miami had all won national titles while Devin was growing up. Devin idolized Florida State star Deion Sanders, but he also admired University of Florida running back Fred Taylor. Devin was familiar, too, with the Miami Hurricanes' rich football tradition, which included winning five national titles between 1983 and 2001.

Miami is just 75 miles from Riviera Beach. Devin wanted to play football close to home, so he chose the University of Miami. His older brother Lenorris was playing football for another school in the Miami area, Florida International University, when Devin committed to the University of Miami in January 2002. Devin told Steve Dorsey of the *Palm Beach Post*:

CROSS-CURRENTS

Read "University of Miami Football" to learn about the big-time football school that Devin hoped to attend. Go to page 49. ▶▶

> **❝I've always felt in my heart that I was going to commit there. It's a big load off of my shoulders.❞**

Devin earned good grades in high school, but his Scholastic Aptitude Test (SAT) scores were not very high. Devin didn't know it at the time, but his low SAT scores would delay his admission to college—and test his commitment to being a Miami Hurricane.

HURRICANE HESTER

In August 2002, Devin eagerly traveled to the University of Miami campus for the start of the new school year. When he reported to the football team, however, Devin was told he was not cleared to play. The university's admissions office was holding up his **enrollment** because of "academic issues." That's when Devin learned his SAT scores were too low.

Devin was stunned to learn the test scores were holding him back. He had taken the test in 2000 and believed his scores were high enough to allow him admission to Miami. The National Collegiate Athletic Association (NCAA), an organization that oversees the athletic programs of many colleges and universities,

When Devin arrived on campus in 2002, he was shocked to learn that he was not eligible to play football. The NCAA had ruled that Devin's grades and test scores were not high enough for him to enroll at Miami.

disagreed. The NCAA's Eligibility Center ruled that Devin was not eligible to play.

Devin was stunned by the NCAA's decision. He returned to Riviera Beach and began wondering if he would ever play college football. He told sportswriter Jorge Milian:

❝When I found out what happened, I went back home and stayed inside the house for two weeks, wondering what to do next. My mom told me that I had to get out of the house and do something. She told me that I couldn't lay around hanging my head.❞

Devin (right) covers a receiver during a practice session. Although Devin had to sit out the 2002 college football season, he worked out on his own to get stronger and faster.

A New Plan

Devin shook off his depression and began a tough workout program. He also began preparing to retake the SAT. Even though he couldn't work out with the Hurricanes, Devin often showed up at the team's practices. Some colleges with lower admission standards tried to lure Devin away to play for them. However, he still wanted to play for Miami.

Miami's coach, Larry Coker, was very impressed with Devin's devotion to a team and a program for which he couldn't play. He told the *Palm Beach Post*:

> **"Devin has been something else. For a kid to stay with us and want to be here this badly says something."**

Devin had to take the SAT four times. Almost a year after he first committed to Miami, he got the clearance to enroll at the school and join the football team. Sitting out a year had been a painful experience, but Devin made good use of his time off. He had grown an inch taller and added a few pounds to his lean frame. Speaking to a reporter, Devin explained why he had been willing to wait:

> **"I knew it was worth it to come here. If I had to wait five years, I would have waited. . . . It was like going to heaven. It's my dream finally coming true."**

Starting Out Strong

During Devin's freshman year, his playing time was limited to returning kickoffs and catching a few passes. He caught four passes for 116 yards and no touchdowns. His longest catch was a 58-yard reception against Louisiana Tech in his first college game. During that game, Devin also gave Hurricane fans a glimpse of things to come with his kickoff returning skills. Devin returned two kickoffs for a total of 73 yards, as Miami rolled to an easy 48–9 win.

One week later, Devin ran back the opening kick against the University of Florida for a 97-yard touchdown. Devin's run was the fifth-longest kickoff return in the Hurricanes' history. Coach Coker was impressed by the way Devin attacked the defense during that kickoff return:

"I think the thing that makes him special [on kickoffs] is that he's going north and south. It's all upfield. He doesn't waste any motion. He's not going left and right trying to juke people. He sees creases and attacks creases."

There was, however, a negative side to Devin's exciting return. After he made it to the end zone, Devin took off his helmet and showed off for the cameras. His antics cost Miami a 15-yard penalty for unsportsmanlike conduct. Even though Miami won, 38–33, Coker let Devin know how unhappy he was about this behavior. After the game, Devin admitted his mistake:

"Now that I think about it, it's not the return that people remember, it's the taking off of the helmet. That's a young mistake that I made. It's not going to happen anymore. I don't want to be labeled as a guy that takes off his helmet."

Ups and Downs

While returning a kickoff in the third quarter of that Miami-Florida game, Devin sprained his right ankle. His injury would cause him to miss the next three games. Miami, however, won all three of those games without him. After five weeks, the Hurricanes were 5–0 and ranked second in the country. Fans and alumni were talking about a sixth national championship.

Devin returned to action just in time for a game against Miami's biggest rival, fifth-ranked Florida State University (FSU). Like the Hurricanes, the FSU Seminoles were unbeaten, so the game's winner would be in a good position to win the national title.

Florida State managed to keep Devin from getting loose and making long returns. He returned just two kickoffs for 37 yards. Devin's team, however, leaped to a 22-point lead before the Seminoles were even able to score. Miami eventually won the game, 22–14.

The next week, Miami beat Temple University to make its record 7–0. The team's winning streak, however, ended abruptly with a 31–7 loss to the Virginia Tech Hokies the next week.

CROSS-CURRENTS

To learn more about the rivalry between Miami and Florida State, read "The Hurricanes and the Seminoles." Go to page 50.

Devin had a good game against the Hokies. He returned five kickoffs for a total of 119 yards, including a 32-yard return, but that wasn't enough to spark the team. Miami's national title hopes ended a week later, when the Hurricanes lost to the Tennessee Volunteers, 10–6.

The Hurricanes closed out their 2003 season with wins over Big East Conference opponents Syracuse, Rutgers, and the University of Pittsburgh. By finishing with a 10–2 record, Miami earned a trip to the Orange Bowl and a rematch with rival FSU. In the big game, Devin returned three kickoffs for 63 yards. Miami beat FSU, 16–14, and ended the season ranked fifth in the nation.

Devin runs with the ball during a Miami game. As a freshman Devin received national attention for his amazing kickoff returns. His scoring helped the Hurricanes win 11 games and finish the 2003 season ranked fifth in the country.

A Strong Second Season

Devin could look back on an impressive freshman year. He ranked sixth nationally in kickoff returns, with an average of 28.7 yards per return, and he led the Hurricanes in total kickoff return yardage, with 517 yards.

Because Devin had enjoyed such a good first season, Coach Coker and his staff began looking for ways to give him more playing time. During the team's 2004 summer workouts, Devin began practicing as a defensive back. There was also some talk that he might have more playing time as a wide receiver.

Since Devin had done so well returning kickoffs, the coaches also wanted to use him as a punt returner. Miami receivers coach Curtis Johnson said that wherever Devin played, he would be on the field a lot:

> **He's that good of an athlete. We just haven't decided exactly where he's going to be. Right now wherever he's needed is where he's going to play.**

When the season began, Coach Coker and his staff decided to use Devin as an occasional defensive back as well as a kick returner. Devin started four games as a defensive back. He usually played when Miami used a "**nickel defense**," a formation that uses five defensive backs to stop opponents from passing. Devin showed he was a good defender by intercepting four passes.

Running back punts and kickoffs, however, was still Devin's biggest contribution to his team's success. His ability to make long returns and score touchdowns earned Devin the nickname "Hurricane Hester." He was also called "Anytime" because he was a threat to score anytime he touched the ball. This nickname was a tribute to Devin's former idol Deion "Prime Time" Sanders.

By the second half of the season, most teams recognized Devin's skills and kicked the ball away from him. Devin still returned three punts and one kickoff for touchdowns, however.

Devin showed his versatility by catching a pass for 25 yards, and he scored another touchdown while playing on special teams. Devin also made a key interception in the Peach Bowl, which he returned for 28 yards. When the University of Florida missed a field

Devin cuts to avoid defenders while returning a punt for a touchdown against Louisiana Tech, September 18, 2004. During his sophomore season, Devin scored six touchdowns and saw increased playing time as a defensive back.

goal in that game, Devin recovered the ball and ran 78 yards to the end zone.

Miami won the Peach Bowl, 27–10, and finished with a 9–3 record. They ranked 11th in the nation. Devin was named to both the Walter Camp and *The Sporting News* All-American Teams as a kick returner. Nationally, he ranked fifth in punt returns, with an average of 17.6 yards per return. On kickoff returns, he was ninth among NCAA players, with a 26.6-yard average.

Junior Year

After such great success, Devin's junior year was disappointing. In the 2005 season, teams were well aware of his ability to break a game

A crowd at the Orange Bowl cheers the Hurricanes as they enter the field before a 2005 game against Colorado. In 2005 Devin played on offense, defense, and special teams for Miami.

open, so Devin was given fewer good kicks to run back. That season, he only returned seven kickoffs for 113 yards. He scored one touchdown. He also returned 22 punts for 312 yards, averaging 14.2 yards per return.

Devin did see more playing time as a running back and wide receiver. He carried the ball 15 times for 94 yards and caught five passes for 55 yards. His longest reception went for 24 yards. He also continued to play as a defensive back, and he grabbed one interception that he returned for 29 yards.

Once again Miami did well enough to receive an invitation to a bowl game. The Peach Bowl, however, turned out to be a low point for both Devin and the Hurricanes. Louisiana State University (LSU) pounded Miami, 40–3. Although the Hurricanes finished with a 9–3 record, their place in the national rankings slipped to 17th.

CROSS-CURRENTS

To learn about how pro teams evaluate some of the top college players each year, read "The NFL Scouting Combine." Go to page 51. ▶▶

The Peach Bowl loss would be Devin's last college game. After Miami's poor performance against LSU, he declared that he would enter the 2006 NFL draft. Devin felt that he had nothing left to prove as a college player, and he wanted a professional **contract** to help provide for his family. In 2004 Hurricane Frances had damaged his family's home in Riviera Beach. More than a year later, the damage still hadn't been repaired. Devin explained:

> **"I felt like this is the right time to come out for me. It was time to take advantage of the opportunity while it was here. I want to play in the NFL and provide for my family."**

A RISKY DRAFT PICK

Despite his outstanding college career, many people considered Devin a risky draft pick. His junior year at the University of Miami had been solid but not great. Even though he played well on offense, defense, and special teams, Devin was considered a talented player who had never established himself at any one position.

Despite those concerns, the Chicago Bears drafted Devin in the second round of the 2006 NFL draft. He was the 57th player chosen. Bears Coach Lovie Smith said he intended to use Devin as a kick return specialist even though Devin had been drafted as a corner-back. Many Bears fans also speculated that Coach Smith would take advantage of Devin's speed by using him as a wide receiver.

Devin Hester poses for the camera, 2006. NFL teams liked Devin's athletic ability, but were concerned that he was not ready for professional football. The Bears ultimately selected Devin in the second round of the NFL draft.

Wherever the Bears decided to use him was fine with Devin. He knew he was ready to play in the NFL. He told *Seattle Times* sportswriter Jerry Brewer:

> **"I was hearing a lot about [how] I wasn't ready. I wasn't going to do the things that I accomplished in college. I heard, 'He's not going to step up to the challenge. He's not going to be ready this year. It might take him three or four years.'"**

After the draft, Devin was eager to show doubters how well he could play.

The Chicago Bears—pictured playing a game at Soldier Field—had gone 11–5 and made the playoffs in 2005. After Devin earned a spot on the team's 2006 roster, he helped the Bears improve on the previous year's record.

Ready to Play

In Devin's first game of the 2006 NFL season, he showed everyone he was ready for professional football by running a kick all the way back. Early in the fourth quarter in a game against Chicago's archrival, the Green Bay Packers, Devin returned a punt 84 yards for a touchdown. The play was a preview of plays to come in Devin's sensational rookie year. Chicago won that game, 26–0, and the Bears began a seven-game winning streak.

Devin had a big role in keeping that streak alive. In the season's sixth game, the Bears played the Arizona Cardinals on *Monday Night Football*. Arizona's record was just 1–4, while Chicago was unbeaten. Many people expected an easy Bears win. The Cardinals, however, played well in the first half and went into halftime with a 20–0 lead.

In the second half, the Bears chipped away at that lead. Finally, with less than three minutes left in the game, Devin caught a punt at his team's 17-yard line. He broke several tackles while weaving through the Cardinals' defense for an 83-yard **touchdown return**. The extra point gave the Bears a 24–23 lead, and they hung on for the victory.

The Bears' hopes for a perfect season ended two weeks later when they lost to the Miami Dolphins, 31–13. The Dolphins kept the ball away from Devin, and he was unable to return any kickoffs. He only had two short punt returns.

Setting Records

Just one week after the Miami loss, Devin embarrassed the New York Giants while tying the record for the longest touchdown run in NFL history. On a missed field goal attempt by the Giants, Devin ran the ball back 108 yards. He accomplished this play by first making the defense think he wasn't going to run.

After picking up the ball, Devin stood at the back of the end zone for a few seconds. As the Giants' defenders began running toward him, Devin acted like he was going to touch a knee to the turf to down the ball. Some of the defenders quit running and started walking off the field. That's when Devin began sprinting down the right sideline. Devin later said:

CROSS-CURRENTS

To learn about another Chicago player who scored many times on kick returns, read "Gale Sayers." Go to page 52. ▶▶

"I probably would have downed it if I saw the defenders coming at me. It seemed like all of them were walking off the field like it was over. So I decided to take it out. It surprised me.**"**

Later, in a game against the Minnesota Vikings, Devin set a new team record with his third punt-return touchdown of the season. He also tied an NFL record for rookies, since it was the fourth touchdown he had scored that year. After picking up the rolling ball, Devin took a step backwards. That gave him time to cut back to the left. He then broke four tackles during his 45-yard return.

Although it was Devin's speed and elusiveness that made the long return happen, he was careful to credit his teammates for making the blocks that allowed him to get loose:

"I had enough time to pick it up and run, and [I] kind of gave a right jab and brought it back around to the left, and my teammates picked up their guys and I got into the end zone.**"**

A Two-Touchdown Game

Only one week after tying the NFL rookie record for returning kicks for touchdowns, Devin set a new mark. In a game against the St. Louis Rams, he ran back two kickoffs for touchdowns.

On the first touchdown run, Devin ran the ball up the middle of the field before quickly cutting to his left. Then, he sprinted down the sideline untouched. In the fourth quarter, the Bears thought the Rams might try to keep the ball away from Devin with an onside kick. To defend against this short kick, most of the Bears players were close to the line, and Devin was the only Chicago player in the end zone.

St. Louis kicked the ball deep, and once again Devin was able to run straight up the center of the field. By the time he reached the Rams' 20-yard line, there were no St. Louis players close to him.

Devin's returns—which covered 94 and 96 yards—ignited a 42–27 Bears win and improved their record to 11–2. That was good enough for the Bears to clinch a playoff spot. After the game,

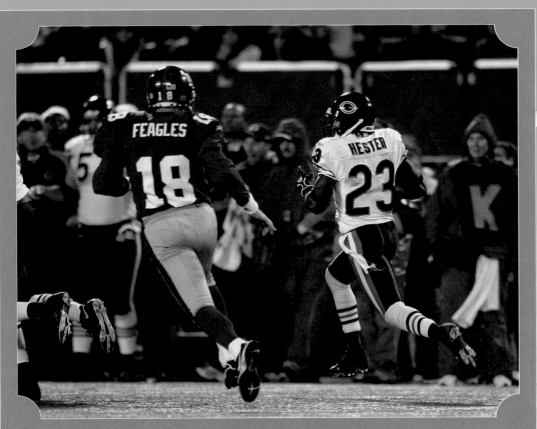

Devin runs a missed field goal attempt back for a touchdown in the fourth quarter of a game against the New York Giants, November 12, 2006. The Bears defeated the Giants, 38–20.

Chicago coach Lovie Smith discussed the impact that Devin had made in his rookie year. Smith told reporters:

> **The story of the game is Devin Hester. It's time that we start looking at him as an offensive player. There are a lot of good offensive rookies in the league making big plays, but who has had as much impact as Devin Hester has in the league as a rookie right now?**

In Chicago's final three regular-season games, Devin returned 10 kickoffs and 11 punts without scoring a touchdown. His longest run was a 28-yard kickoff return against the Tampa Bay Buccaneers.

Bears head coach Lovie Smith appreciated the speed and excitement that Devin Hester brought to the Bears during the 2006 season. The Bears finished 2006 with the best record in the NFC, 13 wins and three losses.

Devin ended the regular season with 20 kickoff returns for 528 yards and two touchdowns. His average of 26.4 yards per kickoff return was the best in the NFC. He also led the conference in punt return average, with 12.8 yards per return. Devin's only apparent weakness was a tendency to fumble. He had eight fumbles in 2006.

The Playoffs

In Chicago's first playoff game, Devin returned three punts and three kickoffs. His longest run was a 20-yard kickoff return. Chicago beat the Seattle Seahawks in overtime, 27–24.

The next playoff game was against the New Orleans Saints for the NFC championship. This time, Devin returned two punts for 24 total yards and three kickoffs for 51 total yards. Chicago rolled to an easy 39–14 win. The Bears were going to the Super Bowl.

In those two playoff games, Devin wasn't able to contribute much to the Bears' wins. That was partly due to field conditions. Both games were played in the rain at Chicago's Soldier Field, and it was hard to run on the muddy turf. The Super Bowl, however, would be played on a dry field at Dolphin Stadium in Miami. That would give Devin a better opportunity to use his shiftiness and breakaway speed.

Making Super Bowl History

Super Bowl XLI featured a matchup of one of the NFL's best offenses with one of the league's toughest defenses. Chicago's opponents, the Indianapolis Colts, were led by All-Pro quarterback Peyton Manning. Manning led the league with 31 touchdown passes.

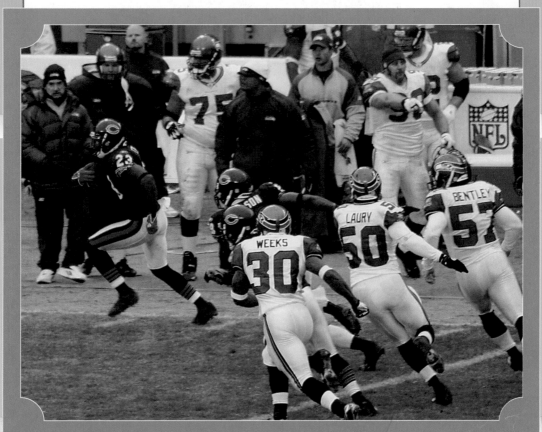

Although Devin could not break a kick return for a touchdown in Chicago's first two playoff games, he still was an effective weapon. Here, he runs a kickoff back 40 yards during Chicago's 27–24 win over the Seattle Seahawks.

Indianapolis's offense had averaged just over 379 yards a game during the regular season.

The Bears defense, spearheaded by All-Pro linebacker Brian Urlacher, had been the best in the NFC. Chicago had held its opponents to fewer than 16 points per game, on average.

When a strong offense meets a strong defense, the play of the special teams often decides the game's outcome. The Colts knew that it was vitally important to stop Devin Hester. In *Sports Illustrated*, sportswriter Peter King outlined the way he thought Indianapolis would try to prevent the speedy kick returner from doing any damage:

Devin crosses midfield, with Colts defenders in pursuit, during the first play of Super Bowl XLI. He became the first player in the NFL history to return the opening kickoff of a Super Bowl for a touchdown.

> **"Colts punter Hunter Smith won't be worrying about his average on Sunday; he'll be more focused on booming the ball high or out-of-bounds so Hester never has an open field. And look for [Adam] Vinatieri, a superb directional kicker, to corner Hester with boots to one or the other pylon. The Colts could also choose to kick pop flies, so when Hester catches the ball, say, at his 20, he'll already be in traffic."**

Surprisingly, the Colts opened the game by kicking the ball right to Devin. That was a mistake they quickly regretted. Devin made Super Bowl history by becoming the first player to return the opening kickoff for a touchdown. After catching the ball near the left sideline, Devin cut back to the middle of the field, then made a second cut to his right. When Devin entered the end zone, three Colts were trying to catch him. Devin's 92-yard return put the Bears ahead, 7–0, after only 14 seconds!

For the rest of the game, the Colts kept their kicks away from Devin. That strategy worked. Devin only had one more kick return, and the Colts won, 29–17.

CROSS-CURRENTS

Read "Super Bowl Kickoff Returns" to find out about other notable returns in the history of the NFL's biggest game. Go to page 53. ▶▶

Honors and Awards

In just a few months in the NFL, Devin had become a full-fledged star. During the season, he was named the NFC's Special Teams Player of the Week three times. He was also named NFC Player of the Month for December. Devin was a finalist in the 2006 Rookie of the Year voting, and he was selected to play in the Pro Bowl.

Devin's teammate Brian Urlacher summed up Devin's record-breaking rookie season:

> **"You never know what he's going to do. . . . The play's never over when he's back there. He's patient. He just catches and he waits and then he takes off. I've never seen anything like it before in my life. I don't play the Madden game or whatever it's called, but that guy is like someone in a video game. He's unreal."**

BECOMING A WIDE RECEIVER

After Devin's All-Pro rookie season, Coach Smith knew that more teams would avoid kicking the ball to him. Because Devin was a scoring threat anytime he had the ball, Smith wanted to find a way to use him more on offense. Smith and the other Chicago coaches talked to Devin about using him as a wide receiver.

In preseason practices, the Bears helped Devin make the adjustment to the new position. They limited the number of new plays he had to learn as a wide receiver to about 15 to 20 plays. Coach Smith explained Devin's role in the offense:

❝It's safe to say he won't play any tight end, he won't play much fullback, and he won't play quarterback.❞

After Devin's explosive 2006 season, the Bears wanted to give the speedy young star a greater role in the team's offense. During the 2007 training camp, Chicago's coaches began training Devin as a wide receiver.

Hands on the Ball

Chicago started its 2007 season with a 14–3 loss to the San Diego Chargers. During this game, Devin didn't catch any passes or return any punts, and he had just one kickoff return for 29 yards. He was stopped, but that would only last for one game.

In week two, Devin returned one punt 73 yards for a touchdown. In a second long return, he brought the ball to the Chiefs' 19-yard line to set up a field goal by Bears kicker Robbie Gould. Devin ran another kick back 95 yards for a touchdown, but this play was called back due to a penalty. Still, Chicago defeated the Kansas City Chiefs, 20–10.

Devin huddles with the offense during a 2007 game. As a wide receiver, Devin caught 20 passes for 299 yards. He scored two receiving touchdowns, on catches covering 81 and 55 yards.

After the game, Devin admitted to the Associated Press that he wanted to score every time he got the ball:

> **"If there's [a returner] who every time he touches the ball [doesn't feel] he can take it the distance, he doesn't need to be out there. I feel every time I get my hands on the ball it's a touchdown."**

Two weeks after the Kansas City game, Devin had his first kick-off-return touchdown of the season in a game against the Detroit Lions. The 97-yard return excited Bears fans, but Chicago lost, 37–27. The defending NFC champs continued to struggle over the next few weeks.

In week six, Devin enjoyed a two-touchdown game against Minnesota. He caught a game-tying 81-yard touchdown pass and returned a punt 89 yards to the Vikings' end zone. Once again, however, the Bears lost, dropping their record to 2–4. Chicago now had already lost more regular-season games than it had in 2006.

Doing His Best

Devin didn't criticize his teammates or his coaches after the team's poor start. He continued to practice hard and do his best in every game. He didn't act discouraged, even when other teams were kicking away from him so he couldn't get the ball.

In a game against the Philadelphia Eagles, Devin didn't have a single kick return, but he caught three passes for 41 yards. Two days after that game, *USA Today* sportswriter Larry Weisman jokingly noted how teams tried to avoid kicking the ball to Devin:

CROSS-CURRENTS

To learn about some other NFL players who made their mark bringing back kicks, read "The Greatest Kick Returners." Go to page 54. ▶▶

> **"If Devin Hester would like to see the football again, he might have to ask a court for visitation rights. Nobody wants to kick to him anymore."**

Finally, in the team's 11th game of the season, Devin broke out. Early in the third quarter, Devin fielded a punt at Chicago's 25-yard line and ran up the left side of the field. On the way to the end zone, he jumped over two Denver Broncos defenders.

Later, with two minutes and 38 seconds left in the third quarter, Devin returned a kickoff 88 yards and scored again. His two touchdowns helped Chicago win in overtime, 37–34.

The win over Denver improved the Bears' record to 5–6. The team still had a chance to reach the playoffs if it could win at least four of its last five games. Instead of putting together a winning streak, however, the Bears lost three straight games.

Devin didn't score any touchdowns in those losses, although he did get the ball a few more times as a wide receiver. In games against Washington and Minnesota, he caught nine passes for 95 yards.

After the loss to Minnesota, sportswriter Peter Dougherty pointed out that when Devin wasn't scoring, neither were his teammates:

"In the four games in which Hester has scored, the . . . Bears have averaged 32 points. In the 10 games in which he hasn't scored, they've averaged 13.8 points."

Chicago closed out its disappointing season with wins against Green Bay and New Orleans—the only time in 2007 that the Bears won two games in a row.

The season-ending game against the New Orleans Saints was one of Devin's best. In a 33–25 win, Devin returned a punt 64 yards for a touchdown and scored another touchdown on a 55-yard reception from Kyle Orton.

Devin was pleased to end the season on a winning note, but he felt the wins should have come more often:

CROSS-CURRENTS

Read "Staying on Top" to learn about other teams that finished with losing records a year after playing for the championship. Go to page 55. ▶▶

"Coming off the season we had last year, we were hoping for better things. But at the end of the day, we left off with a good note. Look at the way we're playing right now. We should have been doing that all season. It's tough."

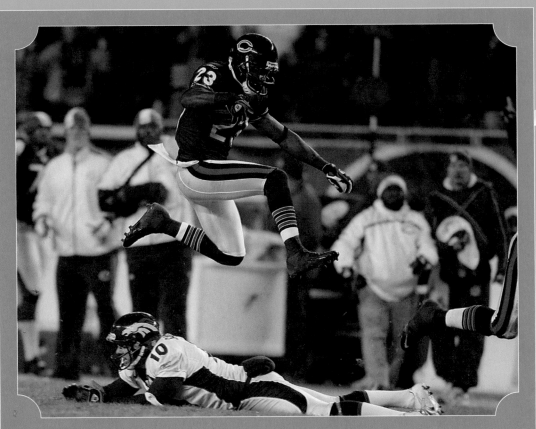

Before Chicago's game against the Broncos, Denver punter Todd Sauerbrun said he was not afraid to kick the ball to Devin. Here, Devin leaps over Sauerbrun on his way to the end zone. Devin scored two return touchdowns that day.

Helping Others

Devin worked hard on the field, but he worked hard off the field as well. Devin has given back to the Chicago community by participating in fundraising events for the charity Bears Care. Since 1995, the charity has raised over $14 million for programs supporting education, youth athletics, medical research, and health awareness.

Devin has also used his success to help the Greater Chicago Food Bank. After he was hired as a commercial spokesman for Campbell's Chunky Soup, Devin arranged for the company to donate 3,960 cans of soup to the food bank. The weight of the donation was equal to the combined weight of Devin and his mother, Juanita.

Support from Family and Friends

Devin credits his religious upbringing, and particularly his mother, for his success. He once told reporters:

> **[My mother] plays a big factor in [my career]. I give her all the credit for the success right now that's going on in my life, and I couldn't have a greater mom than her.**

Juanita believes Devin's religious upbringing helps keep him humble and down to earth. Devin still brings a Bible with him to every game. Juanita explained to sportswriter Larry Mayer:

> **By us being a Christian family, I brought him up a lot in the church. I think that's what keeps him humble. Knowing everything he's gotten—his ability, his strength and things that he can do—all is thanks to God.**

Another person who has helped keep Devin humble and focused is his former idol and now good friend, Deion Sanders. The two met when Devin was in college. Sanders has said he was impressed by Devin's desire and determination to be the best at what he does.

Like Devin Hester, Deion Sanders enjoyed great success and fame at an early age. As a player, however, Sanders was often criticized for his flashy personality and his on-field celebrations. Now Sanders hopes he can show Devin how to handle fame. He talks to Devin about how to manage his money and how to conduct himself when he's in the public eye. Sanders also sends Devin an inspirational text message every morning. He told *USA Today*:

> **I love him. I really love him. I want to correct the mistakes that I made in life through him and not have him make the same mistakes.**

A Bright Future

For Coach Smith, going from the Super Bowl to a losing season was a tremendous disappointment. Still, he is optimistic about his team's future, partly because of the improvements Devin has made as a pass receiver.

While Devin was learning how to play the new position, he did have some problems with dropping passes and running pass routes. These problems were not unusual, however, and Smith was patient. The coach told Peter Dougherty that he expected Devin to have a bright future as a receiver:

"I think [Devin] is a weapon right now. Does he have a ways to go? Yes. He's in the initial stages of becoming a dominant receiver, but we've gotten him more and more time at the receiver position. I think that he has a great future as a wide receiver in the NFL. He's made great progress each week."

Devin waves to the crowd at an ESPN event after the 2007 season. After two great seasons in the NFL, Devin signed a contract extension with the Bears. The new deal would keep him in Chicago through the 2008 season.

"I think the Bears have a lot of faith in me, and they feel that I do a lot of things on the offensive side of the ball, so they rewarded me," Devin said after signing his new contract.

Hester Rule

Devin has already had a great impact on the National Football League. After the 2007 season, the NFL's competition committee considered adopting a new rule. This rule would prevent teams from punting the ball out of bounds. Some writers called it the "Hester Rule" because teams frequently kicked the ball out of bounds when trying to keep it away from Devin. Ultimately, however, the committee decided not to adopt the new rule.

After only two years and 32 regular-season games in the NFL, Devin has returned 11 kicks for touchdowns. That's not counting the Super Bowl touchdown or the touchdown he scored after recovering an opponent's missed field goal. The NFL's all-time leader in touchdown returns, Brian Mitchell, has just two more—13. Nine of those were punt returns and four were kickoff returns. It took Mitchell 13 seasons to achieve that many touchdown returns. If Devin doesn't suffer a serious injury, he is very likely to break Mitchell's record in 2008. After that, there's no telling how far he could go.

When Devin entered the league, he signed a four-year, $2.61 million contract with the Bears. Although that is a lot of money, Devin was underpaid compared to many other NFL stars. Over his first two seasons, Devin scored more touchdowns than anyone else on the team. Before the 2008 season, the Bears rewarded Devin for his great play with a contract extension that will keep him in Chicago through 2013. Under the new deal, Devin will earn at least $15 million. He could make as much as $40 million.

For the next few years Devin Hester should continue to be one of the NFL's most exciting players. He almost certainly will live up to his reputation as a player who can change the outcome of a game—anytime.

The Pro Bowl

The NFL is the only major professional sports league that holds its annual all-star game after the regular season ends. Major League Baseball, the National Basketball Association, and the National Hockey League hold their all-star games in the middle of their seasons.

The first NFL-sponsored all-star game was played in early 1939, after the end of the 1938 season. The NFL champions, the New York Giants, beat a collection of all-stars from other NFL teams and two independent teams, 13–10. This version of the game, with the NFL champion playing a group of all-stars, continued for four years until World War II interrupted the NFL's play.

The all-star game resumed in 1950 and pitted the all-stars of the NFL's American Conference against the all-stars of the National Conference. After the NFL was realigned into East and West divisions in 1953, the game matched up the best players in the East with the best in the West.

That arrangement continued until the NFL formally merged with the American Football League (AFL) in 1970. The game, now called the Pro Bowl, became a matchup between the best players in the AFC and NFC. Since then, the AFC has enjoyed a slight edge. Through 2008, the AFC had won 20 times, while the NFC had 18 wins.

A view of the 2007 Pro Bowl game at Aloha Stadium in Honolulu, Hawaii. In his first Pro Bowl, Devin returned kickoffs for 17, 33, 24, and 23 yards, and had a 63-yard punt return.

Three groups—the fans, players, and coaches—vote on who will play for the NFC and AFC in the Pro Bowl. Each group has one-third of the voting power to prevent fans of one team or one particular player from dominating the vote. Before 1995, only coaches and players were allowed to vote.

Starting in 1951, the Pro Bowl began giving a Most Valuable Player (MVP) award. From 1957 to 1971, the game presented two awards—one for the most valuable offensive back and one for the most valuable defensive lineman. One year later, two MVP awards were given, one to the best offensive player and the other to the best defensive player. Since 1973, however, only one MVP award has been given.

Since 1980, the Pro Bowl has been played at Aloha Stadium in Honolulu, Hawaii. The game has grown into a weeklong celebration. The week before the game, there are numerous parties, an NFL alumni touch football game, a celebrity golf tournament, and a football skills contest.

Some players look forward to the Pro Bowl as a postseason Hawaiian vacation. Other players feel honored to be selected, but they choose not to play, so they can rest and recover from the long NFL season. (Go back to page 6.) ◄◄

Pro Bowl Rules

The Pro Bowl has been called the least intense game on the NFL schedule. Still, there is always the chance that a player might get seriously injured during the game, so the Pro Bowl is played under a special set of rules.

Under Pro Bowl rules, the offense isn't allowed to shift before the ball is snapped. The offense also is not allowed to send a receiver in motion, and it has to have a tight end on every play. The offense can't line up more than three receivers on one side.

To protect the quarterback, the defense isn't allowed to **blitz**. The defense is also required to line up in a 4-3 formation on every play, and it can't use more than four defensive backs to cover receivers. Unlike in regular season games, the quarterback is free to throw the ball away if all of his receivers are covered.

Place kickers and punters are also protected under Pro Bowl rules. The special teams can't rush a kicker during a field goal attempt, on a punt, or during a point-after-touchdown (PAT) kick. A fan watching the Pro Bowl won't see any blocked kicks.

While you're not likely to see any bone-jarring hits during the Pro Bowl, you will see the best players in the NFL play an entertaining, wide-open, high-scoring, end-of-the-season exhibition game. (Go back to page 7.) ◄◄

Deion "Prime Time" Sanders

While Devin Hester was growing up in southeastern Florida, he admired Deion Sanders and closely followed Deion's career as both an NFL star and a Major League Baseball (MLB) player.

Deion first showed his talent as a multi-sport athlete while playing sports at North Fort Myers High School. He was a quarterback and defensive back on the football team, and he was second team All-State in basketball. Deion also was **drafted** out of high school by the Kansas City Royals, an MLB team.

Deion turned down the Royals' offer and accepted a football scholarship to Florida State University (FSU). At FSU, Deion played football and baseball and ran track. His blazing speed in the 100- and 200-meter runs qualified him for the 1988 United States Olympic Trials, but it was in football that Deion had the greatest impact. Deion earned All-American honors, and, during his senior year, he won the Jim Thorpe Award as college football's best defensive back.

After leaving FSU, Deion went on to play both professional football and baseball from 1989 to 2005. During a 14-season NFL career, Deion won a host of honors and awards. He played in eight Pro Bowls and was the NFL's Defensive Player of the Year in 1994. Deion also played in two Super Bowls.

Throughout his NFL career, Deion loved making big plays and being in the spotlight. His love of attention and his ability to run back interceptions and kicks for many yards and touchdowns earned him the nicknames "Prime Time" and "Neon Deion."

Football was Deion's favorite sport, but he also played Major League Baseball (MLB) for four teams from 1989 to 2001. Football, however, kept him from playing a complete 162-game baseball season. Still, in 1992 Deion was able to bat .304 while playing in 97 games for the Atlanta Braves. That same season, he led the National League in triples, with 14.

Playing for the Braves in the 1992 World Series, Deion batted .533 and stole five bases in four games. His play also gave him the unique distinction of being the only person to play in both a Super Bowl and a World Series. After retiring from both sports, Deion returned to the NFL in 2004 to play two seasons for the Baltimore Ravens.

(Go back to page 12.) ◀◀

University of Miami Football

If Devin had been allowed to play for the University of Miami (UM) in 2002, the Hurricanes might have won their sixth national title. That year, the Hurricanes posted a 12–0 record before losing to the Ohio State Buckeyes, 31–24, in the Fiesta Bowl. The double-overtime win gave Ohio State the national title and ended the Hurricanes' 34-game winning streak.

Before that game, the Hurricanes had won national titles in 1983, 1987, 1989, 1991, and 2001. Three of the title-winning teams—the 1987, 1991, and 2001 teams—had a perfect 12–0 records. The 1983 and 1989 teams were both 11–1.

While Devin was growing up in Riviera Beach, the Hurricanes set a National Collegiate Athletic Association (NCAA) record by winning 58 consecutive home games at Miami's Orange Bowl Stadium. That incredible run began in 1985 and finally ended in 1994. Miami's school record streak of never being held scoreless is almost as impressive. From 1979 to 1994, the Hurricanes played 188 consecutive games without being **shut out**.

Although it's been a few years since the Hurricanes have won a national title, Miami has still produced many All-American football players. Four former Miami players—Ted Hendricks, Michael Irvin, Jim Kelly, and Jim Otto—are in the Pro Football Hall of Fame. There are currently over 45 former Hurricane players in the NFL, including Devin.

(Go back to page 15.) ◄◄

When Devin was a member of the Hurricanes, the team played its home game at the Miami Orange Bowl. The university's logo can be seen in the center of the field in this aerial view of the stadium.

The Hurricanes and the Seminoles

Ever since their first game in 1951, the University of Miami Hurricanes and the Florida State University (FSU) Seminoles have had an intense, heated rivalry. During the 1990s, this rivalry became even more intense because both schools were regularly competing for a national title.

From 1990 to 1999, FSU won two national titles while compiling a 10-year record of 109–13–1. During that same span, Miami was 92–26 and won the national title in 1991. Three times between 1991 and 2000, Miami defeated FSU. In all three games, the Hurricanes shattered the Seminoles' hopes for a national title because FSU couldn't kick a field goal late in the game. These three defeats have come to be named Wide Right I, II, and III.

Wide Right I occurred at Doak Campbell Stadium in Tallahassee in 1991. Both FSU and Miami were undefeated, but FSU was ranked number one, while Miami was ranked number two. FSU's Gerry Thomas had kicked three field goals, but FSU was still trailing, 17–16, late in the game. With less than a minute to go, Thomas's final attempt at a field goal went wide right—passing too far to the right of the goalpost to score. Miami held on for a one-point win and finished the year 12–0. Miami then shared the national title with the University of Washington Huskies, who also had a 12–0 season. FSU finished the season 11–2 and ranked fourth in the nation.

Wide Right II happened one year later at the Orange Bowl Stadium in Miami. Once again both teams were undefeated, but this time the Hurricanes were ranked number one and the Seminoles number two. FSU kicker Dan Mowery missed a game-tying field goal when the Seminoles were trailing 19–16. Miami ended the year 11–0, but it lost the national title by losing to Alabama in the Sugar Bowl. Wide Right II was the only loss for the 11–1 Seminoles that year. The year 1992 ended with FSU ranked number two and Miami number three.

Wide Right III occurred at the Orange Bowl in 2000. Late in the game, FSU was trailing, 27–24, when Seminole kicker Matt Munyon missed a field goal attempt that could have sent the game into overtime. Despite the loss, the Seminoles still earned a spot in the Orange Bowl—the bowl game that decided the national title. They lost to Oklahoma in that game, 13–2. That same year, the 11–1 Hurricanes beat Florida in the Sugar Bowl, 37–20, and ended the season ranked number two. The 11–2 Seminoles finished the year ranked fifth in the nation.

(Go back to page 20.)

The NFL Scouting Combine

Every year at the end of February, scores of specially selected NFL hopefuls are invited to Indianapolis, Indiana, where their athletic and mental skills are tested and evaluated. During what is known as the NFL scouting combine, players endure three days of intense scrutiny by NFL scouts, coaches, and executives.

A potential player's fortunes often can rest on how well he performs at the combine. A **mediocre** performance may lower a player from being a first round draft pick to being a second round or lower pick. An outstanding performance can make a previously overlooked or low-rated player a more desirable pick.

Tests for size, speed, and strength include the 40-yard dash, bench presses, vertical jumps, and drills tailored specifically for the player's position. All of the athletes are given a thorough physical exam, and their past medical histories are studied for previous injuries and operations. There is also a drug screening and a personal interview.

The player's mental abilities are tested in the Wonderlic Test. This test is a 50-question exam that covers a number of subjects. Reportedly, only one player in NFL history has ever scored a perfect 50 out of 50 on the test. That fact, however, has never been confirmed. Most scores range from the mid 20s to the upper 30s.

(Go back to page 25.) ◀◀

Linebacker Jordon Dizon loosens up before running the 40-yard dash during the 2008 NFL scouting combine. At the annual combine, representatives of NFL teams test the speed, strength, skills, and intelligence of top college players.

Gale Sayers

Four decades before Devin Hester was drafted by the Bears, another member of this Chicago team was exciting and delighting fans at Soldier Field by returning punts and kickoffs for touchdowns.

Gale Sayers joined the Bears in 1965 after being a two-time All-American at the University of Kansas. Sayers' rookie season was one of the greatest in NFL history. He set an NFL rookie record by scoring 22 touchdowns his first season. One of these touchdowns came on a punt return, and another one came on a kickoff return. The other 20 touchdowns came from running and catching the ball. That made Sayers one of only a few NFL players to score touchdowns four different ways in one season.

Sayers's first-year return averages were 14.9 yards on punts and 31.4 yards on kickoffs. In a game against the San Francisco 49ers, Sayers tied a longtime NFL record by scoring six touchdowns in one game. Sayers's accomplishments earned him the NFL's Rookie of the Year Award.

Sayers followed up his sensational rookie season by leading the NFL in rushing yards the next year. In 1966, he gained 1,231 yards in 14 games while averaging 5.4 yards a carry and scoring eight touchdowns. He also returned two kickoffs for touchdowns.

In his third season, Sayers caught fewer passes and ran the ball less. Still, he averaged 4.7 yards per carry. Even though he only had 16 kickoff returns, Sayers took three of them all the way back for touchdowns. Unfortunately, knee injuries in 1968 and 1970 took away Sayers's blinding speed.

In 1969, Sayers led the NFL in rushing for the second and final time. He had 1,032 yards rushing and scored eight touchdowns. Despite his achievements, however, the Bears had a dreadful 1–13 season.

Sayers retired after the 1971 season. Since then, he's been named to the NFL's 75th Anniversary All-Time Team and the NFL 1960s All-Decade Team. Sayers still holds the NFL record for the highest career kickoff return average, 30.56 yards per return. He also holds the record for the most touchdowns from kickoff returns, with six touchdowns. In 1977, at age 34, Sayers was inducted into the Pro Football Hall of Fame, which is located in Canton, Ohio. He became the youngest player to receive this great honor.

(Go back to page 29.) ◀◀

Super Bowl Kickoff Returns

Although Devin Hester was the first Super Bowl player to return an *opening* kickoff for a touchdown, he isn't the first in Super Bowl history to return a kickoff for a touchdown. That honor belongs to Fulton Walker of the Miami Dolphins. In Super Bowl XVII (1983), Walker ran a kickoff back for a 98-yard touchdown against the Washington Redskins.

No one has ever run a Super Bowl kickoff out of the end zone for a touchdown. Desmond Howard of the Green Bay Packers came the closest, with a 99-yard return against the New England Patriots in Super Bowl XXXI (1997).

Jermaine Lewis of the Baltimore Ravens has the shortest Super Bowl kickoff-return touchdown. While playing against the New York Giants in Super Bowl XXXV (2001), Lewis ran a kickoff back 84 yards for a score. All other kickoff-return touchdowns have been between 92 and 99 yards.

A quick score always gives a team a boost, but the eight kickoff-return touchdowns in Super Bowl history usually haven't affected the game's outcome. Five of the eight times, the team scoring the touchdown ended up losing the Super Bowl.

No player has ever made more than one Super Bowl touchdown on a kickoff return. Devin could have a long career ahead of him—he might set another record and become the first to make more than one.

(Go back to page 35.) ◀◀

Green Bay's Desmond Howard holds the record for the longest Super Bowl kickoff return. In Super Bowl XXXI (1997), he also set records for most punt return yards (90) and kickoff return yards (154), and was named the game's MVP.

The Greatest Kick Returners

It's difficult to name the greatest kick returner in NFL history. Is it the player who has gained the most yards on kick returns, or is it the player with the highest average yardage per kick return? Is it the one who has the most kick-return touchdowns, or is it the one with the most Pro Bowl appearances? While no one kick returner can be singled out as the best, several players can be listed among the top.

Billy "White Shoes" Johnson got his nickname for wearing stylish white football shoes instead of the traditional black cleats. He was nearly overlooked by the NFL because of his small size—he was 5-feet, 9-inches tall and weighed only 170 pounds—and because he played college football at a small NCAA Division III school.

The Houston Oilers took a chance on Johnson, and in 1974, they made him their 15th round draft pick. Johnson showed the Oilers he was worth the risk by running back seven kicks for touchdowns in his first four years with the team. Johnson played until 1988 and was selected for the Pro Bowl three times. He was named as the kick returner on the NFL's 75th Anniversary Team and 1980s All-Decade Team.

Brian Mitchell is the NFL's all-time leader in both kickoff return yardage, with 14,014 yards, and punt return yardage, with 4,999 yards. He's also the league's all-time leader in kick-return touchdowns, with 13. Nine of those were punt returns and four were kickoff returns. Mitchell enjoyed his best seasons when he played for the Washington Redskins from 1990 to 1999. He's been named as one of the 70 greatest players to play for the Redskins.

Eric Metcalf is just behind Mitchell with 12 kick-return touchdowns. He still holds the NFL record for most career punt-return touchdowns with 10. While playing for seven teams from 1989 to 2002, Metcalf led the NFL in punt-return touchdowns four times and played in three Pro Bowls.

Travis Williams had a short but brilliant career while playing for the Green Bay Packers from 1967 to 1971. Williams had five kick-return touchdowns in 62 games. He still holds the NFL single-season record for the most yards per kickoff return, with an incredible 41.1-yard average in the 1967 season.

Among active players, Dante Hall stands out. He's had 12 kick-return touchdowns in eight seasons and will probably pass Mitchell and Metcalf in that category before he retires. Deion Sanders, Gayle Sayers, and, of course, Devin Hester, are also ranked among the best kick returners in NFL history.

(Go back to page 39.) ◀◀

Staying on Top

In professional sports, reaching the top is difficult—but staying there can be even harder. There are a variety of reasons for this. First, opponents have no trouble getting pumped up to play a defending champion; everybody wants to beat the best. Second, winning a title requires intense dedication and focus. Many athletes find it harder to make the necessary sacrifices after they get a championship ring, and champions have to deal with more distractions, such as increased media attention. Success can also breed dissension, as players with big egos move to take credit for the team's triumph. In addition, free-agent stars tend to go where the money is best, so owners typically must be willing to pay high salaries in order to keep their championship teams intact.

The NFL is no exception. Many teams have played in the Super Bowl only to have a dismal season the following year. In February 2007, for example, the Chicago Bears played in Super Bowl XLI, but they suffered a losing record the next season, finishing at 7–9. The same thing had happened to the Philadelphia Eagles after their appearance in Super Bowl XXXIX: the Birds managed to scratch out just six wins during the 2005 season.

Both teams that played in Super Bowl XXXVII posted losing records and failed to make the playoffs the following season, 2003. The defending champion Tampa Bay Buccaneers staggered to a 7–9 record. The Oakland Raiders fared even worse: the 2002 AFC champs got pushed around like chumps, managing to win only four games in 2003 and tying several other teams for the worst record in the league.

The list goes on. The St. Louis Rams played in Super Bowl XXVI in 2002 but had a losing record the next season. The year before, the New York Giants suffered a 7–9 record after appearing in the Super Bowl.

But NFL free falls began long before the tribulations of these recent Super Bowl participants. In fact, the penthouse-to-doghouse storyline goes back almost to the beginning of the big game itself. The Green Bay Packers won Super Bowls I and II but then saw their dynasty abruptly end. Green Bay went 6–7–1 and failed to make the playoffs in 1968.

Another team that made NFL history suffered a similar fate. The Oakland Raiders became the first wild card team to win an NFL championship when they defeated the Philadelphia Eagles in Super Bowl XV. But that triumph was followed up with a disappointing 7–9 regular-season record in 1981, and the defending champs failed to make the playoffs.

(Go back to page 40.) ◀◀

1982   Devin Hester is born in Riviera Beach, Florida, on November 4.

1992   Devin's mother, Juanita, is seriously injured in a car accident. She remains bedridden for nearly two years.

1994   Devin's father, Lenorris Hester Sr., dies of cancer.

2002   Devin scores 26 touchdowns in his senior year at Suncoast Community High School and is named to various All-American football teams. At the CaliFlorida Bowl, Hester returns a kick 85 yards to score a touchdown. He signs a letter of intent to attend the University of Miami, but his admission to the school is delayed because of low SAT scores.

2003   After retaking the SATs, Devin is cleared to attend the University of Miami. As a freshman, Devin leads Miami in kickoff return yards. He is ranked sixth in the nation for the average kickoff return yardage, with 28.7 yards per return.

2004   Devin scores four touchdowns on kick returns (three punts and one kickoff). In a game against Louisiana Tech, Devin becomes the first Miami player to score two touchdowns on punt returns in a game. In the Peach Bowl, he returns a blocked punt 78 yards for a touchdown against the University of Florida. On defense, Devin leads Miami in pass interceptions, with four.

2005   After a disappointing junior year, Devin declares his eligibility for the 2006 NFL draft.

2006   Devin is a second-round pick of the Chicago Bears and the 57th player chosen overall. In his rookie year, Devin helps the Bears to an NFC Championship by returning five kicks (three punts and two kickoffs) for touchdowns. Devin ties an NFL record for the longest touchdown run by returning a missed field goal attempt 108 yards for a touchdown.

2007   In Super Bowl XLI against the Indianapolis Colts, Devin becomes the first player to return the opening kickoff in a Super Bowl for a touchdown. In the Pro Bowl, Devin has a 63-yard punt return. The Bears begin training Devin as a wide receiver. He has two touchdown receptions and averages 15 yards per catch. In the 2007 season, Devin sets an NFL single-season record by returning six kicks (four punts and two kickoffs) for touchdowns.

2008   Devin plays in the Pro Bowl for the second time; signs a contract extension with the Bears.

2002   *Parade Magazine* High School All-American; *USA Today* First-Team High School All-American; Florida Class 3-A All-State First Team; MVP of the CaliFlorida All-Star Game; SuperPrep rating as the number one college football prospect in Florida and number six in the nation.

2003   Ranked sixth nationally in kickoff return average, with 28.7 yards per return; wins the Big East Conference indoor long jump title in track and field.

2004   Named to the Walter Camp All-American Team as the best kick returner in college football; named kick returner on The Sporting News All-American Football Team; First Team All-Atlantic Coast Conference (ACC) kick returner; named as the ACC Special Teams Player of the Week three times.

2006   NFC Special Teams Player of the Week three times; NFC Player of the Month in December; finalist for Pepsi NFL Rookie of the Year; NFC Pro Bowl team.

2007   NFC Special Teams Player of the Week four times; ESPY Breakthrough Player of the Year Award; NFC Pro Bowl team.

Books and Periodicals

Freedman, Lew. *Chicago Bears: The Complete Illustrated History*. Stillwater, MN: Voyageur Press, 2008.

Frisch, Aaron. *The History of the Chicago Bears. NFL Today* series. Mankato, MN: Creative Education, 2005.

Lawrence, Andrew. "(69) Devin Hester." *Sports Illustrated*. September 3, 2007. p. 85–86.

Woods, Bob. *NFC North, the Chicago Bears, the Detroit Lions, the Green Bay Packers, and the Minnesota Vikings*. Chanhassen, MN: Child's World, 2003.

Web Sites

www.devinhesterautographs.com

Devin's official Web site has a photo gallery, biographical information, and information on buying sports memorabilia signed by Devin.

www.nfl.com

The official Web site of the NFL has Devin's latest stats and biographical information.

www.chicagobears.com

The Chicago Bears official Web site tells where the team will be playing and offers information on Devin. The site also has a Kid Zone.

http://hurricanesports.cstv.com/

The University of Miami Hurricanes' official Web site offers information on the university's football program as well as other athletic programs.

blitz—a defensive play in which one or more defensive backs charge behind the line of scrimmage and attempt to tackle the quarterback or force him to throw the ball as quickly as possible.

contract—an agreement between two parties. In the NFL, these agreements are between players and teams and involve decisions on how many years the player will play for a specific team and how much the team will pay the player.

draft—the process by which NFL teams select new team members from among the nation's top college football players.

enrollment—the process by which students sign up, are accepted into, and pay for college courses.

field goal—a three-point score that is made by kicking a ball over the crossbar of a goal post and between the post's upright bars.

fumble—the act of dropping the ball or having it knocked out of a player's hands so that the player and the player's team lose possession of the ball.

idolize—to admire, without seeing flaws or faults.

intercept—to steal a pass away from its intended receiver.

juke—to make a deceptive move to force a defender out of position so the defender can't make a tackle.

kick return—catching a ball that the opposing team has kicked or punted and carrying it to the end zone in an attempt to score. A **kick returner** is a player who performs this task.

kickoff—a kick that puts the ball in play at the start of a game, at the start of the second half, or after a score.

mediocre—of moderate to low quality.

nickel defense—a defensive formation that uses five defensive backs to cover the opponent's receivers.

prospect—a young player who has shown good athletic skills and who is expected to play well on future teams.

punt—a kick in which a player drops the ball and kicks it before it hits the ground. If a football team has not gained 10 yards in three downs, it may decide to punt on fourth down. This gives possession of the ball to the opposing team farther away from the punting team's end zone.

pylon—a short, flexible orange foam marker that marks each of the four corners of the end zone.

sack—a play in which a defensive player tackles a quarterback behind the line of scrimmage.

shut out—kept from scoring any points.

special teams—the groups of players who handle plays that involve kicking, including kickoffs, punts, and field goal attempts.

touchdown return—a score that is made when a players catches, or fields, a kicked ball and carries the ball into the end zone. These types of scores are also called kick-return touchdowns, kickoff-return touchdowns, or punt-return touchdowns.

wide receiver—an offensive player who is positioned the farthest from the ball and who must catch a ball thrown by the quarterback.

page 7 "I'm not amazed any. . ." Mike Dodd, "Hester's Two TDs Spark Bears to Crucial OT Win," *USA Today* (November 26, 2007), p. 6C.

page 9 "Hester is the quick. . ." Mike McAllister, "Battle of the Return Kings: Hester vs. Cribbs," ESPN.com (February 9, 2008). http://sports.espn.go.com/nfl/news/story?id=3237727

page 9 "I have been around. . ." Mike Mulligan, "Hester's WR Transition a Game of Give and Take," *Chicago Sun-Times* (June 2, 2008). http://www.suntimes.com/sports/mulligan/982266,CST-SPT-mully02.article

page 11 "It was probably. . ." Tom Pedulla, "Big Returns on Bears' Investment," *USA Today* (January 31, 2007). http://www.usatoday.com/sports/football/nfl/bears/2007-01-30-hester-cover_x.htm

page 12 "I was 11, . . ." Adam Duerson, "Devin Hester," *Sports Illustrated* (December 3, 2007). http://vault.sportsillustrated.cnn.com/vault/article/magazine/MAG1114237/index.htm

page 15 "I've always felt. . ." Steve Dorsey, "Hester Will Play for UM," *The Palm Beach Post* (January 22, 2002), p. 1C.

page 17 "When I found out. . ." Jorge Milian, "Hester Reports to UM; 3 Others Fail To Qualify," *The Palm Beach Post* (August 4, 2003), p. 8C.

page 19 "Devin has been. . ." Milian, "Hester Reports to UM," p. 8C.

page 19 "I knew it was worth. . ." Milian, "Hester Reports to UM," p. 8C.

page 20 "I think the thing. . ." Jorge Milian, "Hester Losing Patience," *The Palm Beach Post* (September 30, 2003), p. 11C.

page 20 "Now that I. . ." Milian, "Hester Losing Patience," p. 11C.

page 22 "He's that good. . ." Omar Kelly, "Hurricanes' Hester to Play Where He's Needed Most," *South Florida Sun-Sentinel* (August 1, 2004), p. 11C.

page 25 "I felt like this. . ." Omar Kelly, "Early Entry a Gamble for Hester," *South Florida Sun-Sentinel* (April 28, 2006), p. 13C.

page 28 "I was hearing a lot. . ." Jerry Brewer, "Bears Rookie Hester Is a Paradox," *Seattle Times* (February 1, 2007). http://seattletimes.nwsource.com/html/sports/2003552386_brewer02.html

page 30 "I probably would have. . ." Tom Canavan, "Bears 38, Giants 20," Associated Press and *Yahoo Sports* (November 13, 2006). http://sports.yahoo.com/nfl/recap?gid=20061112019

page 30 "I had enough time. . ." Andrew Seligman, "Defense Leads Bears to 2nd Straight Title," *Deseret News* (December 4, 2006), p. D7.

page 31 "The story of the game. . ." "Bears Profit on Hester's Returns, 42-27," NFL.com (December 11, 2006). www.nfl.com/gamecenter/recap?game_id=29068

page 35 "Colts punter Hunter Smith. . ." Peter King, "Showdown Showcase," *Sports Illustrated* (February 5, 2007), p. 47.

page 35 "You never know. . ." Larry Mayer, "Hester Wins Second Straight Player of the Week Award," ChicagoBears.com (December 13, 2006). http:www.chicagobears.com/news/NewsStory.asp?story_id=2796

page 36 "It's safe to say. . ." Andrew Lawrence, "Devin Hester (69)," *Sports Illustrated*, (August 28, 2007). http://vault.sportsillustrated.cnn.com/vault/article/web/COM1058239/index.htm

page 39 "If there's not one. . ." Associated Press "Defense, Special Teams Enable Bears to Win," NFL.com (September 16, 2007). http://www.nfl.com/gamecenter/recap?game_id=29223

page 39 "If Devin Hester would. . ." Larry Weisman, "Four Downs: Bears' Hester Got His Kicks on Offense," *USA Today* (October 23, 2007), p. 6C.

page 40 "In the four games. . ." Peter Dougherty, "Hester Dilemma Awaits," *The Capital Times* (December 22, 2007), p. C1.

page 40 "Coming off the season. . ." Rick Gano, "Devin Hester's 2 TDs for Bears Send Saints out of Playoffs, 33-25," Associated Press and *Yahoo Sports* (December 30, 2007). http://ca.sports.yahoo.com/nfl/recap?gid=20071230003

page 42 "[My mother] plays a big. . ." Larry Mayer, "Hester credits His Success to His Mother's Influence," ChicagoBears.com (November 13, 2007). http://www.chicagobears.com/news/NewsStory.asp?story_id=4074

page 42 "By us being. . ." Mayer, "Hester credits His Success to His Mother's Influence."

page 42 "I love him . . ." Pedulla, "Big Returns on Bears' Investment."

page 43 "I think [Devin] is . . ." Dougherty, "Hester Dilemma Awaits," p. C1.

page 44 "I think the Bears . . ." Quoted in "Bears' Hester Gets Reported $40 Million Extension," *USA Today* (July 28, 2008). http://www.usatoday.com/sports/football/2008-07-27-2494179194_x.htm

Numbers in **bold italics** refer to captions.

Jeff C. Young is a graduate of Ball State University, and he lives in North Port, Florida. He has written over 25 books for young readers. His book *Bleeding Kansas and the Violent Clash Over Slavery in the Heartland* won the 2007 Spur Award from the Western Writers of America for Best Juvenile Nonfiction Book.

PICTURE CREDITS